Hewn

Hewn

poetry

Heather Angier

STEPHEN F. AUSTIN STATE UNIVERSITY PRESS
NACOGDOCHES, TEXAS

Stephen F. Austin State University Press
Nacogdoches TX. 75962.
sfapress@sfasu.edu

Book and cover design by Emily Townsend
Cover art by Erik Linton: "900-year-old Juniper Tree"

ISBN: 978-1-62288-219-9
First Edition

For girls who suffer from scoliosis

Hewn

CONTENTS

Idiopathic

your vanity bores me—
        it's this flexible body
        flexible body
now interesting me.
watch how
watch how I muscle you. You
        adolescent   you
    always   checking
        bedroom mirrors
feeling diseased
        diseased

            how
            these
        bones
        bones
            slow
            move
            trip
            and
            bend
            bend
            you
            ever
            so sli-
            ghtly
            slow

        how
        physical
        physical
    I grow
        for you
            this
            more
    interesting
        curvature

O   knuckled spine
        knuckled spine
        wristed rib
    elbowed hip.

Crooked

Except, there was no tower
or rampion
      garden witch
snaking up
the highway, up past
      the battered mailboxes
  and hidden
firehouse, up through
      tangled manzanita—

I can smell it still—
      mushrooms
  fern
    and wood-smoke
fog at the top—my Tamalpais.

Just eleven—
  braced
      chaste hips
    strapped in and shut up—
no man yet, either
     nuzzling about
girl blonde
   rangy hair, grown
  to hide it—
day   night   years passing
no steps out
   no window
  no door for the locked
up, the gently
     tortured girls.

Back Brace

slipping on a dead rat
          hitting the corner of stair
crippled to the floor
—a crying, awkward girl.

          generations of
                    discarded appliances
                              fill the upstairs:

Uncle Lester's phony leg props open a window.
Hosmer's wire spectacles rest on the dresser.
Aunt Algae's black shawl hangs from a crutch.

(voices downstairs
float up
through the floorboards

          she's adjusting,
                    poor thing…)

          Aunt Fanny's wicker wheelchair
          at the foot of the bed.
                    Nell's orthotic shoe
                    wedged under the desk.

all the false teeth
tucked into drawers.
                    it's enough, she
                              stares at the shelves.

Cricket Trick

And there appeared Frances
      ghost-pale, beside me—
the star-pocked night
      thick with crickets:

It was 1849—she began,
      and all of us hungry.

We crossed the plains—
      Indians watching, put
our iron pot on the fire.
      When it bubbled, they came
closer, threw in fistfuls of crickets.

Well, what?!—she slapped
      her knee, hard.
The next night?! We picked
      dead cricket from our teeth!

Milwaukee Brace

hermit crab
picking across rock
in a black turban shell

feral pig trapped
in the night
apple orchard

blue lizard slips
into cement
stair crack

rattlesnake
holed up
on the trail

quail panicking
in the quiet
gray fog

raccoon snorting
fist in a jar
under the trailer

blind mole
unearthed

airless

Crossing the Gila
c.1850

Wagon wheels
        starving dogs

oxen—tongues
swollen, overburdened

      sinking, sinking
Even the sun

swallowed whole—
        the shifting sand

opening hot
toothless mouths

dreams
are sinking   Bury it all

      to survive—
books, glass bottles

medicine   Mark it—
bones, bones

in stark moonlight
      Reach Camp

Salvation—*swallow*
soft beans,   hot meat

clear water   *sink*
into beds—bellies

swollen   twisted
and aching   This

is the moment
my heart

sinks   this is
when he turns back

swallowed
       in blinding wind

holds the shovel
grits his teeth   and digs

Salt

no ship sunk   no drowning
prince
                    just my little sister
          slapping gray ocean

begging the witch
                    for a fish's tail

I'll sell you my soul

                    the doctor, he
told her,   "swim
          —no brace—
          as long as you like"

he talked of gravity
          her shifting
                    bones
my hair

the treading cold
                    brings her in
I can only wait
          with this towel, I can only
watch her walking
          towards me
                    fog-silent
on stinging legs

          my tongue

Straight Talk

I'm supposed to encourage her.

I know this when the doctor winks,
tugs at his white beard. Leaves
me to answer one question:

"What's it like—wearing a back brace?"

Twenty-three hours. Every day.
Four years.

I'm tempted by metaphor.
the tortoise has its shell

I want to give her a severe look.
it wears you

Or show her my graying scars.
it will cut you

I want to hide her.
find another way

Her secret girl-eyes fight.

I think of the hours she'll cry
trying on all the fat pants at Ross—
tell her

patience

If Topographers Wore Back Braces

here,
jutting purple
on each hip bone—
a rare bruise

and here, across
the stomach, this
temperamental plane
covered by rash and welt

and here, just under
this arm, a cut
opened daily—the thinning

map of my skin
now softer than talc

Frances
c. 1850

By glowing embers
  limp rabbit still
gripped, the moon-
       drenched babies
  now asleep
in the stretched
  canvas wagon—
maybe she could hardly
    form the words:
He took the baby,
William! So I aimed—
     maybe her voice
her hands   cracked
             trembled
   like prairie grass
under the catastrophic
          stars—
   maybe he set
down the pelt-
soft   rabbit   gentle
   in the settling
  smoke—maybe
he held her, his own
  trailing hands
      also unsteady

Braceless

leap, girl
        into the trees—

stretch, girl
     in tangles
       of wood,
  hanging moss

grin, girl
   feel the grace
of your crooked back—

        touch your toes,
      girl

now,
stay like that
         kissing
      those knees

Emma's Gray Wedding Dress
Stockton, CA 1870

100°F   rising   hands   ready   the wood   stove   now   the boilers

steaming   hands   burning   scrubbing   the boards   now   rough   soap

hands   raw   stinging   now   comes   the mangle   wringing   pins

hanging   comes   the irons   hot   coal   heavy   hands   comes   scarring

now   aching   so long   doctor   shirt   ruffles   my hands   now

holding   this   farmer   gray   dress   comes   rain   now   maybe

the mud   won't   show   so much

Prognosis

choked
        I've got spines
            coming out of my head

the doctors   they
        don't have the words
                    I need—

have heart failures
        of their own   have

left the room, accidentally

            shut the door
            on my tongue

Anesthesia

       the girl cursed—
a needle prick—yes,
  blood dropping, and   oh
       when she fell—the rock
hard ground, medieval
  sleep—a violent vine
                wresting
  barb and bone,
       spine and thorn—raging
  inside   her motionless
    body, eyes closed
the moving world—
                        stilled.

Chinese Dairy Hand
Lodi, CA 1885

        waving
          a cheese knife, comically
yelling

       Me kill you! Me kill you!

              sweat trickling

chickens flapping, children

          squealing, flushed
          out of hiding

and everyone laughing until

        the last milk can is washed

and moonlight spills
        its sorrow—

the scent of her skin remembered—

chased nightly,
        dear opium.

Pea

    the sheet pulled
            meticulously
irons out the wrinkles—
      relieves somewhat

this knifing bed

it's the same old story
there's even a storm

though—this is no castle
      but a hospital
    twelve stories high

and I'm no real princess
    blackened blue
bedded down—well,
           really

there's not even a pea

gleaming and
  lodged
      under this
    painstaking

mattress, stitched
blanket, clot of

pillow

Sister

The defroster in the Mazda broke.
I rub circles with my hands,
don't get lost, drive dangerously.

Ghost-pale—she's hooked up
to monitors, spits up shaved ice.
The morphine is wearing off. She is wracked—
doubles up in her sleep. I watch her
eyelids quake, veins like delicate
lines in a cracked eggshell.

Her room is above a panorama of Oakland lights.
Below, an advertisement for Oriental Nails.
Yesterday—a picnic. Point Reyes sandwiches:
tomatoes, baguette, brie. It was cold.
We walked along the ridge. Sun on gray water.
The horizon lit up like a scar.

My sister can't have flowers in Intensive Care.
Tomorrow she'll be moved. In four days, she'll stay awake
for almost a half hour. I'll feed her ice chips, comb
her hair in the blue light.

I like her nurse.

Rags

Poor shirt, flat out
on the table.

The scissors I'm holding
reflect something precise.

I snip up its back—
hear tiny ribs cracking.

Down its front,
I think about blood.

Sorting through its strewn scraps,
I feel myself

hesitate, then gather up
a presentable pile.

Canaries

That was the screen door—
                    rusted hinge,
          sound of visitors.
Juaquin Murieta,
          wanted dead or alive,
stands politely—clears his throat.
          He studies her children
     playing with a wet dish towel,
                    a wooden spoon.
Handing him a sack of vegetables—
          the widow pretends
she doesn't notice his scar-
          whipped, brooding heart.
          It is summer—hot.
The room swells with understanding.
     Children say when he left
          wild roses tamed
                    horses collided
and a flock of gold coins
          dropped like yellow birds
to the dusty floor boards below.

Harrington Rods

If it were a dream
I'd be running, wounded
on the border—

to my left, twisting madrones.
To my right, a rigid
city construction zone.

Some days I'm made soft—
fleshy. Other times
I'm hooked metal.

I'm like that tree at Pantoll—
the one with a rusted trail sign
cut into its trunk—

the one hikers stop under, marveling
how the body swallows it, how
incredibly, it survives.

Swim

Tomales Bay
is shark water. Regardless,
          you want in, although
      one cold touch
renders you blind,
          scrambling for   the drift-
                              wood raft.
Out here, breathless
          body dripping, you try
calming yourself, peer
                  into a luminous
      bay—discover bells pulsing
          tentacles threading
and silent.   No use
                  counting them, dear—
      they surround you
and this raft is anchored. So,

          forget the sharks—
                  you must slip quietly
      into saltwater
                  gloss jellyfish.

Arthur's Drowned—

       his   body
laid across

the stained   backseat
tail lights   glowing

      the grave sun
still lowering—

the horizon   the water
all horribly   red

who can look   oh, look
everything   everything's

red

Undertow

In a cold
drag of ocean

we lost
our footing.

The salt water
rose

when you
clutched me

so I kicked
you away.

See,
little moth?

I once tried
to explain,

I am not
myself

strong
enough.

See how
I find you

treading linoleum
by the stove

how I can
only

hold you
so long

then swallow
sea

Sitting in Bed

I assess the damage of this day—

tell him
small lists:

aneurysm
tumor
varicose veins.

I show him an elbow,
stick out my tongue.

I point to the arch of my foot.

His strong arm
reaches for me

Come here, broken girl.

Donkey Skin

it stayed where it fell
   oh heavy   oh dank
        rough
      at my ankles—

the morning I shed
   my donkey skin
the forest sparkled

     raindrops hung
   like lanterns
from steaming pines—
    lit my hands
as I reached up
       its throat
and ripped
      its jaws apart—

   only then did
      my true body
glow   scar white
   and step away
        cautiously

so as not to disturb
its blunt-yellow teeth.

Rosewild

mailboxes and cotton house dresses   window screens   wood chairs   grass   spectacles
shot guns   hair pinned into tidy buns   platters   garden spigots   soda pop   white
roses   straw hats   books   drawers and ribbons   hard dirt paths   false teeth
tomato plants   the Victrola   chickens   baby clothes   salt licks   smooth braids
rust   jams and jellies   wheel barrows   glass straws   dull knives   Chinese silks
hay and sunlight   pickles   apron strings   swinging gates   climbing roses   piano
keys   black walnuts   the pump house   oak   suspenders   rat traps   barn green
rafters   carved mahogany   slanted floors   cracked leather   rakes   nests and eggs
yellow roses   tire swings   thermometers   leaves   cigarettes   handkerchiefs   cats
dust and grape vines   velvet   thorns   chipped saucers   pigs   wicker   coats and trousers
pasture   blooms   oranges   cows   sheet music   wagon wheels   glowing porch
lights   button jars   bamboo   pomegranates   silver hand mirrors   black widows   possum
dusk   cobwebs   dark tree branches   fog   fences   porcelain dolls   perfume
tricycles   pink roses   swallows and poppies   wedding rings   irrigation ditches   metal
buckets   blue sky   dents   crates   moonlight   stacked wood   peaches   ladders
and pressed glass   figs falling   pink naked ladies   the secret staircase   cookie tins
sheep   clotheslines   stars   ink bottles   sprinklers   soft lamp light   bedspreads
wash tubs   potato chips   cake stands   stray dogs   creaks and doors   wind-up clocks
the claw foot tub   carpet   red roses   dry toast   grizzly bear skins   top hats   ghosts

Tucumcari

reinvent a word, drive
into a KOA and pitch a tent in August rain.

hold a can of beer
and ask a diamond question.

notice the enormous jowled toad puddled
the cow flare cow nostrils behind weathered fence.

say under a blue sagging tarp
little rubied, *yes*.

Wedding on Tamalpais

I wanted her violent death
erased from this place

but, honey, twenty years
         have past
    and it remains

Damp silk,
         thistle and oak
      lured us all here
   to witness our love—but
         oh,

clever flies.

Like memory, they cling
to our ceremonious bodies

hover in a murderous clutch
above

—this inconsolable ground.

Champagne

Your suit was baggy
and my shoes were all wrong—

but the mountain was itself.
Pale stars lifted, effervescent

above the darkening forest;
a harvest moon hung

antique white. I remember
how you waited patiently,

everyone smiling and cheering
when I finally ran out

to kiss you, electric flashes
lighting our way.

Honeymoon

It's terrible—this habit
of reading in such hot places
books set in snow.

Gruskenka drinks champagne.
Mitya shouts his love.

Pausing to watch you
dive for wedding rings,
I shoot tequila, bite
lime, lick salt.

Blue and yellow butterflies flit.
Purple bougainvillea climbs.
It's going to rain.

Delirium settles.

Aunt Fanny Goes to Sacramento
Influenza, 1917

She must have regretted it deeply—*if only*
she had boarded the train alone.

She should have known he'd hop on up,
still dressed in morning coveralls,

impulsive grin flashing—
Heck, darling! Don't cry!

She probably thought on it obsessively,
the strange details of it—

the fresh smell of animals   *if only*   clinging
hay strands   *if only*   his muddied boots

dumb fly

Tuber

Sleepless and hungry
I stand in dark kitchen: eat

from recycled yogurt container
one organic   homegrown   baby red

leftover   wrinkled potato and
congratulate myself—this moment

I waste nothing. 2:03 a.m.

Nell

has grown old.

She swells   hangs   hums
mmm-hmm bless you.

She sits by the window
in her dark Morris Chair, cradles
penny-cold hands, rubs fingertips
smooth, opens her milk blue eyes.

Nell no longer hears
rats rolling walnuts in the walls—
no longer sees bald
light bulbs that swing.

She has two black shoes, one
metal leg brace. Six hooked canes.

Nell looks out the window—

wild oranges
drop and tumble outside.

Pregnant

    the acacia is singing
trumpeting
bloom

and little Ruby's in heat—
    sniffed out and humped
  in the pod-heavy
shade

      then, there is
this wild moon
         fat yellow
and balmy

listen,

I'll say to him,
changing

Aquafina©

Hunched naked, I'm retching
into the blue soup pot
Jay placed at the foot of our bed.

Holding back my hair,
my moonstruck body, he's awed
by your force.

No bigger than a thought—you
already bring me to this ground,
wincing and grinning

how lucky I am, how
I want you, how can

bottled water taste bad?

Poppies Blooming

This is not romantic.

The air is artificial, the light florescent.
That suggestive tropical plant—a fake.

It's not going well.

"Relax, relax!" the doctor all but shouts.
"Look at Monet!"

I feel myself tense.

Monet is in the corner cringing—
his painting's a poster, tacked to asbestos.

The windows don't open.

But wait! Monet is getting up and trying
to say something, like: "Hang on, you're hurting her"

and "There still remains this issue with the light."

One Hundred

Its sure pink feet
crossed the dusty rug
clawed up the coverlet—
bit her gray-old lip, that rat.

The children insist,
as anyone would,
she finally leave
the old place.

Sunlight casts
mute-gold rectangles
to the sloped bedroom floor—
tell me, what does it take

to die at home
chest barely rising, calm
inside a dream-scent—

roses, walnuts, milk

Happy

The sun didn't shine brighter.
The sky wasn't terribly blue.
No one was taking photographs
or holding up signs.

It was just August, a Tuesday—
still damp from swimming, wriggling
like fat pups, each of them
snuggling into us, their soft tongues

licking my arms.

Let Down

all night
    the room
filling: *milk*
       milk *milk*
floods
    our floating
        bed
 breasts
streaming *milk*
    our baby's lips
pale   blistered
    by daybreak
the room
     overflows
 milk
     sunlight
flooding
  night   our eyes
        wet
   flowing
 milk *milk*—
gratefully,   love
     let down

Nature

And then there's you, Mr. Shiny-
Shoes and Ms. All-Business. Why

separate yourselves from me?
What's the big hurry?

Fine, fine. You eat with a fork
and say *excuse me*. Come tomorrow,

trapped in a startling
elevator, your wild eyes

will again search mine. It's then—
just another sighing mother

adjusting her leaky bra—
I'll shrug, as if

it doesn't matter,
mouth: *it's okay,*

I can feed you all.

China King Buffet
Lodi, CA

Tea cups poised,
we ask about
the silk painting—

two golden birds perched
on a blossoming bough.

Teaching Chinese children
in public schools, she explained,
was once outlawed in San Francisco.
So, after the bell, Margaret hitched up
her skirts—taught in the street.

The painting was a gift
from her students.

One sip and we understand—
even sugared
sometimes tea tastes bitter.

Squirrel

imagine
  our astonishment
      oh my!
walking the kids to school
      through milky fog
the very moment
  I was thinking
what will become of me?
  feeling motherhood
            consume me
      I lost myself
when a hefty green pinecone
          from towering branches
    fell—struck my head
          the sky is falling
instantly knocking me
      back   to my senses

Yard Duty

not stars—
        but more
    planetary—orbiting out
        across wide swaths
of blacktop, each
    sweat glittered body
        sparking
            laughter
under a punishing sun—
    and it's miraculous
            (*understand?*)
no one here is falling
    or colliding—every
            hurtling child
somehow protected
    by a simple gravitation
                to play

Gobstopper

I watch his heart
     harden—
          each school day
  pushed up against the others,
layers so packed—
       it could break jaws.

If he hides it for later
    I'm afraid
        he'll forget
  he put it on the bookshelf
between Amulet and Tintin—

or worse,

       that he'll find it
      stuffed in some pocket
all covered in lint,
    and then accidentally
     drop it—
          brittle star
exploded on the blacktop.

If only I could carry his heart
    for him   safe
      in my animal-mouth
    licked and sucked
      like a bruise—each
tempered coating
    dissolved to the last
soft, chalky center—

sugar sugar, teeth aching.

Antique

I think of her sometimes
on certain occasions—

an anniversary, perhaps
when my ring hits

a raised glass with a ting
and our sparkling laughter

holds up the ceiling—or maybe
on a dim autumn night

having just cut my finger,
blood catching

under its tight band—the kids
shrill in a hot trade

of Japanese Erasers—and
I can see myself

becoming her, somehow
repeating the same

household tasks—wiping up
breadcrumbs

and vomit. So that
I want to ask her—if she too

grew disappointed, in love
with a man who drank

hard. Ah, but there
I am again—standing

in front of that antique
shop in Georgetown, the window-

reflected buses passing me by
while I gaze at its glittery display—

wondering if the ring will fit me
better or worse

than the woman
who had worn it before.

Interstate 80

There is a bleak road ahead
sun-beaten and glaring.

There are tire scraps in the ditches
threadbare and strewn.

There are crows careless in Nevada—
each one, a burden perched

in the silent arms of a bent tree.

Anger

Blown in like a cloud
of billowing pollen—

see how it carries on
through the wheezy streets

and spreads—the autumn
cobwebs hung

maniacal yellow.
Our bloodshot eyes

and constricted throats
are stinging, sore with it—

it covers our windshields
and house steps—

so fine a dusting
children stop and spit—

scratch their names in it.

Furniture

Strange, as if possessed—
        their carved feet

thud on wood floors
   like restless dogs.

Arthur collected the furniture—
       each mahogany piece

meant for a home
        he never built.

There should've been photographs—
      a woman at the secretary

or children lounging with books
      on the old horsehair couch.

Arguments should have erupted
over whose turn it was

to wind the Victrola
        or set the table. But no,

   everybody knows
        he was too young

to drown. It's a grief
      we still carry—

look how we still lug
     his furniture

   house to house;
each generation

inheriting the same
        settling sorrow, each

cumbersome heirloom
    instructing the children:

Lift with your knees! Watch for corners!
Check the water before you dive!

Ghost Town
Bodie, NV

Nothing prepares a man
for love's oppression—
not even the sudden apparition
of a shunned Chinese maid
in his bed, dead winter—
a century after her suicide.

It wouldn't matter
if you stopped loving me.

You would still wake
in a sweat, feel me
straddling you—ribs,
heart, lungs aching.

Look how my mouth
and tongue already press
against yours—ghost silent
and you no longer breathing.

Psithurism

Listen—
it once lulled me to sleep:
                    the forest
          an ocean, through
and through   the open windows
          but now that I've left
the memory of it
                    just keeps me awake.
Maybe it's the longing I long for—
              open windows
                    swaying nights
the dark hulking trees
                    bending and bowing
to the first stirrings of love.

Ink Blot

When we saw the contents of the wooden box displayed, we were curious. *We were!* There was a stack of old, yellowed bank statements from the 1800's. *That was interesting!* There was a personal letter and we read that, almost blushing. Other things, too. But, the dingy paper scrap blotted with William's ink pen? ... Well, we laughed out loud. *We couldn't stop ourselves!* Only it hurt her feelings. *We could tell!* Oh, but it was absurd, don't you see? *She held it so tenderly, with such reverence—the paper scrap!* We imagined the good doctor in his brown duster, digging heels into the sweaty flanks of his horse, off to treat the sick gold miners. *We did!* "Christ Almighty," he muttered, turning to go.

Giraffe Sex

There is an art to distraction. Like magic.
Every staged waterfall confirms it, every strategically placed rock.
Ironically, this has always made you feel confined, admit it.

Children now gather by the manufactured creek, small mouths agape.
The giraffes are moaning—no, bellowing—frothy, drooling, in wild ecstasy.
Blushing mothers fuss with babies. Fathers wander off, smirking.

But the children stare and stare, alarmed or amazed—depending.
Until one deft mom winks at you, breaks open a box of zoo animals:
cookie, anyone?

Even you forget yourself.

Nest

Hattie is crying
for the baby robins
she found covered in ants
last Saturday.

She would not leave
their twisted-pink bodies
(laid out for viewing
on the backyard pavers)
until we troweled
a matchbox grave in the ivy.

At her age, I also memorized
ugly deaths—fingered
dried, peeling deer skin
stuck to skulls and jaw bones
before I flung them back
to the throbbing forest.

No wonder Hattie's crying—
her small practicing hands
burying me under blankets
on her down-soft, suburban bed—

falling,
    falling
our nested hearts,
transparent,
plunge.

Moving Virginia to Senior Housing

It's like that morning
of the big storm
at the wooden Live Oak School
when the cooped up children
gathered on the front porch
breathing out clouds
in the wet air.

The wind gusted up—
catching the huge oak
that had stood for years
on the corner of Cherokee Lane.

Its leafless branches
trembled and shook
until it finally lifted out
of the soaked ground
and stayed like that—
suspended—
dirt clods dropping,
the splayed roots exposed

as shocked
as the children who saw it.

Snow Globe

I like to cup the glass
in my warm hands

put it right
to my eyes

and peer in at us
transfixed

in a moment
we left behind

shaken people
now frozen

bone chips
whirling—

and should my heart
feel reconciled

I set it down—
that which will

never be ours again.

Vulture

A tough old bird will watch
from fettered bed
children finally entering
her room.

Bare walls
having closed in
months ago, hunger
has set in—a starvation.

Bald, but for a few stray hairs.
Nose beaked.
She'll circle conversations—
then scavenge their lives
for carrion news.

You'll see, as the visit ends
her blood-slick head will emerge
from their opened bodies—her keening
eyes glazed, neck stretched

hissing, grunting in satisfaction.

Love Lessons at Mini Golf

The castle drawbridge opens,
then closes, much like a heart.

In mid-afternoon swelter,
I watch flirty teenagers

whack golf balls
against shutting doors.

Helicopters hover
like giant dragonflies

over stagnant moats
and clogged freeways.

No magic here, but
notice the lesson:

if you want into the castle,
you'll need some skill, some timing,

some luck.

Pancreatic Cancer

Auntie Pam gathered her things,
spread them around her bed quilt

and watched us carefully pick and choose—
dust floating in the windowed sunlight.

We ate Mediterranean sandwiches from Panera,
placed small vases and teacups, glass straws

and hair pins into awkward piles, watched her
carefully nibble a sodium-packed pickle spear.

From her: a tiny box I now fill
with my children's lost baby teeth.

Rattling and blood-crusted, they are
not as perfect as you'd think.

Don't tell Ben about the pickle,
she said, perking up.

Compost

The camellias are selling it;
each lusty bloom—
a gorgeous heart
throbbing—*love, oh love*

think of it:

wrapped in quiet
moonlight—I trace
your graying sideburns,
the crow's feet stamped
across your face—and listen
to our old, sold hearts
thumping.

Well, what, so what
that flowers fade, drop
one by one, some-
times in pairs,
to the garden below.

This is love, they yell
falling, *love*

think of it:

all those open hearts
on open hearts—heaps
and heaps of them—
eventually raked, shoveled
into bruised, soggy piles

and look at us
all the while
vaguely aware
something lovely
can still grow from it.

Anniversary

Strong,
      this craggy
            cliff—

where nude oak
          twists
  twines   roots

into cracked
      starlit rock—

look at us, love

   gripped
         and silent
each holding
         the other

so as not to fall—

the reeling ground
      almost rising

Hewn

as in   a slumped house   boards, nails loose
                       paint peeling

     or   its women
          bearing down
        in fig-dark rooms

but also   the packed dirt paths   now overgrown
                         interstices of light

and   a deformed girl   cut open, bones
           disturbed

   all of it   *all of it*

       imprinted   so don't worry
              our DNA
         will remember   even if
we forget

Acknowledgments

I wish to thank the editors of the following publications, where these poems first appeared (some in earlier versions):

Caduceus: "Straight Talk"
Cider Press Review: "Salt," "Pea"
Green Hills Lantern: "Compost"
Literary Mama: "Pregnant," "Yard Duty"
Miniature Magazine: "Tuber"
Pirenes Fountain: "Aquafina©"
Poetry East: "Snow Globe"
So To Speak: "If Topographers Wore Back Braces"
Switchback: "Anger"
The Dirty Napkin: "Prognosis," "Undertow," "Rags"
The Poetry Box: "Gobstopper," "Compost"
The Sow's Ear: "Crooked," "Straight Talk," "Harrington Rods"
Whale Road Review: "Giraffe Sex"
Zyzzyva: "Idiopathic"

Chapbooks:
Dancing Girl Press: *Crooked*
Finishing Line Press: *Nest*

Thank you to my family, especially Jay, Finn and Hattie

photo by Finn Johnston

Born and raised in Northern California, Heather Angier is currently pursuing happiness as an ordinary mother who steals spare moments to read, write and publish poetry. She has a Master of Fine Arts in English and Creative Writing from Mills College. This is her first full-length book.

CPSIA information can be obtained
at www.ICGtesting.com
Printed in the USA
BVHW03s0218210918
528152BV00001B/5/P